Following The Fading Light

Light

A collection of things unsaid

Aarika Sehgal

Made with ♥ on the BookLeaf Publishing Platform
www.bookleafpub.in
www.bookleafpub.com

Dedication

To all the Seraphic Souls finding their purpose, I hope you stumble across your true self

Preface

This book began as a quiet answer to the feelings I couldn't quite voice. There are moments when words fail us, when even the closest person can't fully understand what we feel. I found myself carrying thoughts and emotions that never quite fit in conversations, and poetry became my way of giving them form. Writing has been my passion, a place where I can turn the intangible into something real.

I believe that each of us has a part of ourselves that we struggle to frame, words that sit unspoken, hidden deep inside. This book is for those moments. My hope is that, as you read, you'll find echoes of yourself here. I want you to feel seen, understood, and maybe a little less alone in your thoughts.

This book is for anyone who has ever felt stranded in their own emotions, for those who long for words that feel like home. May you find a part of yourself within these pages, and may it remind you that you're not alone on this journey.

Welcome to the words I could never say, now given light.

Acknowledgements

First and foremost, my deepest gratitude goes to all the individuals who have inspired my poetry.This book is a collection of those raw, intimate moments, woven together to echo the shared feelings of humanity.Sometimes more time with some people feels less.To mumma,papa,suhu,bhootu,megha mam I will forever be grateful of you.

I invite readers to feel a part of this journey. I believe the power of this book lies in its honesty—by diving deep into the core of what we all experience, I hope readers will find themselves reflected in these words, much like I found pieces of myself in these emotions shaped in this work.

In a world with countless poetry books, I believe mine stands apart because it dares to explore the intricate beauty in everyday feelings, the unspoken moments we all carry. The cover, with its minimalist yet evocative design, resonates with the simplicity and depth found in the poems themselves. It's meant to capture attention not with grandiosity, but with quiet reflection—mirroring the internal nature of you verses within.

This book is for those seeking connection, for those who appreciate the subtlety of emotions, and who find comfort in vulnerability.

 I want this acknowledgment, along with every poem inside, to reach those who long for words that feel as though they've been pulled from their own hearts. Thank you for choosing to walk this path with me.

I. Was my faith a mere whisper?

Oh God! My faith in You, was a child's pure cry,
Dear Lord! I mourned, but You passed by.
When I begged for You to make things right,
Was it an elder sister's curse, or just my plight?

Was growing up not sunshine's gleam,
But lost in shadows of a dream?
Be honest—did You hear my plea?
Or was Your silence just meant for me?

I held my faith with fingers tight,
But it slipped away into the night.
Was it there or just a lie,
A fleeting whisper passing by?

Yet I'll wait for you, like Romeo for Juliet's hand,
Or like sleepless souls for dawn to land.

II. The Girl Who Loved the Sun

This is to the girl who loved the sun,
But one day found its light had come undone.
Her eyes, once bright, now pained by the gleam,
Tired of the weight, of every dream.

Yet somehow, expectations lit her way,
A newfound strength in all they'd say.
From being a fragile doll on display,
To losing love's touch, it slipped away.

When I see her now, I wonder still,
Did you have dreams, waiting to fill?
You didn't deserve the trials you faced,
Loving me before love found its place.

I wish I'd confessed what you meant to me,
You were my light, though I couldn't see.

III. Forever Your Little Girl

You used to sing me songs to make me sleep,
'Cause I'm not your classic lullaby to keep.
That little girl who always had it all,
With a dad who'd go beyond, big or small.
Anyone can be a father, but you're my dad,
And saying I'm your daughter makes me glad.
Sometimes I wonder how you see the world,
What thoughts you think, what emotions swirl.
I try to guess your expressions, but then,
I stop, 'cause it's hard imagining when
You hide so much behind that gentle smile,
Carrying burdens, mile after mile.
I'll always be that girl, waiting at the door,
No matter how tall, I'll look up even more.
You seem tough, but inside you're pure gold,
A heart that loves, more than words can be told.
Thank you for the sacrifices you made,
So I'd see the world, with courage displayed.
You showed me strength, through all you've done—
Like the world belonged to us, since day one.

IV. Once a kalopsia, then remained an eccedentesiast

She didn't know when it all started,
how, overnight, she began hating herself.
She lost pieces of herself, searching for something she
couldn't name,
becoming less of who she was and more of... it.
Silence screamed louder than ever,
her eyes staring back in the mirror, wishing they could
disappear.
Birthdays became days of regret,
and reality blurred—were these nightmares or brutal
truths?
She forgot the warmth of joy,
the feel of things by heart, the look of sunlight.
Was this the death of childhood,
or the birth of poetry?
The lumps in her throat twisted into tight knots,
until her voice echoed in the void,
forgotten, while she remained the kalopsia—
the beautiful illusion she couldn't see.
And so, she became the eccedentesiast,
the one who smiles to hide it all.

V. Whispers Left Behind

What those orbs definitely weren't were words,
The way they confessed, not truths, just blurred.
Simply making my eyes blurry, yet it wasn't hope,
I wonder if it was your gleam that helped me cope.
I was already drowning; they just asked, *"How was the fall?"*
They sparkled once like stars—now a white dwarf, so small.
Maybe someday, somewhere, they'll find their shine,
Hollow, yet with secrets buried deep in line.
The gaze never softened, so you could never see,
Their secrets untold, hidden just from me.
I know they should have seen it all coming somehow,
But the only question that arises is how.
Before the final goodbye, just teach me to let go,
Then I'll walk past you like strangers who'll never know.
But they'll always remember, though time may fade it,
We were so close, *we almost made it.*

VI. Back to Page One

To those friendships I'll always cherish,
To the ones who've been there, unwavering and true,
I can't imagine life without all of you.
For saving me from solitude,
And teaching the art of sarcasm, too.
For making me laugh when I thought I couldn't,
And translating the mumbled, untold language of my
sleep.
Our friendship isn't perfect—but it's real, it's enough,
With silly promises, crazy times, and memories to love.
We're truly partners in crime,
And even when I'm overbearing, you handle me just
fine.
As a kid, I wondered if Winnie the Pooh's friendship was
real—
Thank you for showing me it is.
One day, we might not see each other as often,
One day, we'll miss each other and feel invisible tears
fall,
One day, we'll realize that places never mattered—people
did.
And we'll feel the words of Winnie the Pooh ring true:
"Goodbye...? Oh no, please. Can't we go back to page one

and do it all over again?"
To all those friends who became family.

VII. Death's Gentle Promise

They say death is dark, a shade of gray,
A toll we all are meant to pay.
But what if my death holds another sight,
Not the end of dreams but a dawn of light?
They say the heart's a beast in a cage,
Bound by sorrow, fear, and rage.
But what if death could break those chains,
Freeing the soul from life's remains?
What if death were a child's delight,
A lullaby sung in the softest night,
Where peace enfolds like a sweet embrace,
And every wish finds its own place?
They speak of heaven's gentle gleam,
A tapestry sewn from quiet dreams,
While hell, they say, brings fire and moans—
But what if hell just heals the unknown?
Angels, they say, are hope's bright strings,
And demons, angels with broken wings.
Who'd fear death, with its calming hue,
When some souls die before life is through?
So let me lean on death awhile,
For living may just beguile.
If life's the dream, a fleeting spree,
Then death is truth—the final key.

VIII. Where Dreams Dare to Dwell

If dreams could be real, I'd force my lids tight,
And tell my eyes to roam in fantasy's light.
I'd dream of a world in colors rare,
Lost by the water, with beauty laid bare.
I'd wonder if all that has slipped me by,
Could be mine once more beneath the sky.
I'd dream of a childhood, a better release,
To live without worry, and rest in peace.
In this moment, regret would flee,
And I'd savor the seasons, finally free.
Oh, laughing at last as I learn to adore,
The self I neglected, but now, no more.
A world where promises always stand,
Where peace blooms wide across the land.
A place where no one sweeps or hides,
Where love is true, and trust abides.
For hearts are denied what they long for deep,
So I'll dream of a world where wishes keep.
But it's time to wake and face the day,
Will dreams survive or fade away?
Should I open my eyes, confront what's true,
Or close them once more and drift anew?
Choosing the reality

Or keeping the trust issues on the bay
I shall decide now can i see my castles of imagination
shatter anyway?

IX. When Healing Hurts

A child who yearned for arms to hold,
In warmth and safety, a story told.
Yet I wore a smile, a mask so bright,
To make others feel that all was right.
The understanding child, I'd take it all,
Embracing the burdens, I'd never fall.
Growing up loud, an extrovert's guise,
But my inner thoughts stayed locked inside.
No one could grasp the depths I'd feel,
So I remained quiet, hiding the real.
But they found solace in the girl who cared,
With a listening ear, my heart always bared.
Having known betrayal, I kept secrets tight,
Helping them heal brought me sheer delight.
As they grew stronger, I'd start to see,
That perhaps I was more than just me.
A therapist friend, my role became clear,
Yet I longed for someone to hold me near.
I painted my joy with colors so bright,
But life wasn't easy; I struggled in light.
Carrying burdens, I wore them like cloaks,
With laughter and kindness, I masked the upspoke.
Surviving the days, not truly alive,
In helping others, my own pain would thrive.

So, I buried my troubles, deep in the ground,
Making their stories a part of my sound.
In this dance of healing, I learned to survive,
But deep down, I wondered—could I truly thrive?

XI. Beyond Goodbye

I left bits of myself in everything I loved.
In the way we used to be,
in the way things used to be—
God, how careless I was.
Those times when nothing seemed to matter,
we changed like the tides,
forever shattered.
I watched the sun slowly sink into the ocean.
Can I remind you?
Promises aren't one-sided,
but even those memories don't belong to me anymore.
Who wants to be safe, anyway?
Let's be shattered,
because in those broken pieces,
I can still feel your presence.
I wonder if even destiny wept,
tearing us apart.
There was never an end,
nor will there ever be,
but in the parting, you took pieces of my soul—
some I kept,
and others, I fear, will always remain yours.

XII. A Fragile Definition of Love

Why do I destroy everything I love?
Maybe this time was different.
If only I'd known it was just an illusion.
You were my favorite mug of coffee, the one I held too tightly,
afraid it might slip and shatter.
Instead, it broke in my hands.
In that moment, I realized how flawed my definition of love was.
Yet, I kept holding the pieces just a little too long.
They cut me a little too deep,
but I wished they could have stayed with me just a little more.
Expectations existed because belief existed—
the hope that if I could sacrifice so much,
couldn't they give just a little?
But people aren't homes.
They aren't residents of castles.
They are like drowning—
an experience that pulls you under,
and somehow, you learn to love the taste of the salty water.

XIII. The Promise of Green Fields

The stranded boat floats in the middle of nowhere,
all alone, with the water still and lifeless.
The sun has been setting for years but never fully sinks.
There comes a point in life when you realize you aren't
truly alone.
Overthinking becomes your closest companion,
stress a regular guest,
anxiety a relentless lover.
You long for someone, because even to yourself, you're
now a stranger.
Life stops being about "living"—it's only about surviving.
But no one questions the soil, the trees, or the flowers,
so why question yourself?
They say nothing lasts forever,
so maybe this moment of drifting won't either.
Perhaps the sun will set one day,
and I'll find peace at last.
No one really understands, and maybe they never will.
But you just have to love yourself enough,
to hold yourself close on sleepless nights.
And if that's still not enough,
we'll meet again in the fields of green, my love.

If the sun sets there we shall not regret
Cause at least-the view was worth it

XIV. The Burden of Glass

They say never trust a mirror;
it can make you feel worthless and amazing all at once.
But was it always this way?
Don't we suffocate it?
Every morning, asking it to judge us.
What if it wasn't meant to be like this,
but we shaped it, molded it into something unforgiving?
Maybe the mirror felt joy once,
when we returned to it, giving it purpose.
But when we left, who was it then?
What if it longs to comfort you when you cry,
to whisper, "You're perfect, darling. Flaws don't matter."
Perhaps it's become like a toxic parent—
too damaged to heal itself,
passing that damage on to others.
And so, it went on,
ruining everything it was meant to reflect.

XV. Ink in Place of Tears

This failing body of mine—
it feels harder to hold on now.
Overreact? No, dear, I don't do that.
Explosions of noise in my mind,
whispers that remind me of every stumble, every failure.
People aren't much different,
their eyes looking at me like I'm a criminal.
No one wants pity; even that has its own weight to bear.
Surrendering was never an option;
if I did, I'd just be labeled "drama."
Crushing hopes beneath each step,
life was never easy.
Some days, I'd scream without a sound,
fighting battles no one else could see,
learning that silence could be its own kind of shield,
even if it left scars no one else could feel.
I don't understand—I just don't.
When did failure stop cutting so deep?
But then, words became my way out,
my silent scream on the page.
And so, I bled on paper.

XVI. A Heart Left to Ache

It was my heart that felt the numbness first,
But I gave my eyes no time to weep.
I filled my days with ten different things,
Hoping to drown out thoughts of you.
I convinced myself I was too happy to be sad,
But when silence fell, when no music played,
And all the tasks were done,
I stilled for a moment, and a tear slipped down.
I'm not even sure what I miss anymore—
The way I felt by your side or simply you.
No one is there to wipe my tears now,
To hold me like you used to do.
Every laugh feels just a bit hollow,
Every joy somehow incomplete.
I carry you in these hidden tears,
A quiet ache only you could ease.

XVII. For My First and Greatest Cheerleader

You were the one who caught me through every fall in childhood,
Holding me close as I sobbed, shielding me with your love.
You scolded anyone who dared raise their voice,
Loving me in a way no one else ever could.
You dreamed of us traveling the world,
Sitting beside me as we drove, proud to be my grandpa.
Even now, I miss you deeply.
Watching others celebrate with their grandfathers, I feel the pang of envy.
I wish I could relive those moments with you—
My biggest cheerleader, rejoicing in my smallest triumphs.
Your scoldings never felt harsh; they were a reminder of your care.
The world feels lesser without you in it.
Memories are a gift; they let me feel your presence even now,
But videos can't capture the depth of reality.
That last call, the one you couldn't answer—
I mourn not just what was lost, but all that could have been.

I will always be your doll.
Just wave back when I look toward the sky.

XVIII. For My Dumbos

My guiding lights, I love you more than you know,
Till the world's end, our universe will remain.
I wonder if you'll always be there,
But if you try to run, don't worry—I'll twist your ear!
Maybe I became a little overprotective,
But it's only because I had no one and wanted to be
someone for you.
I hope life feels brighter with me by your side,
Even if, at times, I might smother you a bit.
Please don't feel hurt when I yell—I never mean it,
Know I'll always be here, no matter what.
Don't keep things bottled up, share them with me.
Life won't be perfect, but together, we'll make it better.
There were moments I felt like nothing mattered,
But then my silly self thought of you.
I don't want you to carry the burdens I've held;
Be yourself, without the weight of holding on.
Live the life you want, and know that your sister will
always try her best for you.
I love you, my dumbos.

XIX. More Than Love: A Tribute to My Grandma

Grandma, the one who felt more than love,
I came running to you even for my smallest needs.
You have always been my companion,
No matter what, always pampered me.
I hope we go clubbing together one day,
Always being the person I gossiped about everyone to.
I wish we do many such adventures together,
'Cause more is less with you.
Life is to click many crazy pics with you,
I love you sooo much.
You're my safe place, my forever guide,
In your laughter and hugs, I find my pride.
With you, every day feels brighter and true,
Life's sweetest blessings all wrapped up in you.
You're my heart's keeper, my joy, my friend,
The one I know I'll love to the end.
May our memories grow and our laughter ring,
For with you, Grandma, life's a beautiful thing.

XX. Sisterhood Beyond Friendship

More than a friend you were to me,
Scolding me over mistakes I made,
Holding me while I cried,
Teasing people till every end,
Later regretting that if we continue we will end up in hell,
But hell would seem better with you.
I have not known you since a decade,
But you surpassed being a headache.
Thank you for making me believe that all friendships are not toxic,
Thank you for being the older sister I never had.
I will always look up to you,
After any minor inconvenience, I will be on my way.
I am very proud of you,
For whatever you do, consider me as a shadow of yours.
To cherishing life with you, I hold you dear,
Through laughter and tears, you bring me cheer.
In moments of doubt, you light the way,
With you by my side, I'm here to stay.

XXI. Lost in the Season's Glow

It's that time of year we're supposed to celebrate,
With happiness and colors filling the air's weight.
Life becomes more joyful than the everyday,
But why, I wonder, don't I feel the same way?

No excitement stirs in my veins like before,
The thrill and the music—I feel them no more.
It just feels like another holiday to endure,
Except I'm forced up to decorate, unsure.

I see the lights that used to bring cheer,
Now they glow faintly, yet warmth isn't near.
Memories linger of laughter and song,
Yet in this quiet, I no longer belong.

Some people made it feel alive and bright,
But they're gone now, fading out of sight.
Maybe I'm drowning too deep in myself,
Lost in my own world, ignoring all else.

A season of joy, a world dressed in light,
But all I feel is a hollow, endless night.
Maybe it's me, or maybe times have changed,

But the spark feels distant, and my heart estranged.

The world dances in a vibrant array,
But I watch from afar, feeling so gray.
The magic once there now slips through my hand,
Leaving me lost in a once-familiar land.

XXII. Following the fading light

In the quiet dusk, a light begins to wane,
A distant glimmer in the growing rain.
I follow its trail, though it fades and bends,
A journey that pulls, but never ends.

Once bright and strong, it led me through,
Guiding my steps in a world I knew.
But now it falters, dim and slight,
Leaving shadows where there once was light.

Each step I take, it slips away,
A fleeting warmth, a ghostly ray.
Yet something in me cannot let go,
Chasing a spark that's sinking low.

Maybe it's hope, or a fear of the dark,
That makes me follow this dying spark.
But as it fades into the night,
I lose myself, following the fading light.